better
together*

* This book is best read together, grownup and kid.

 **akidsco.com**

a
kids
book
about

a kids book about

friendship

by Duncan Cambell
in partnership with Friends of the Children

A Kids Co.
Editor Emma Wolf
Designer Jelani Memory
Creative Director Rick DeLucco
Studio Manager Kenya Feldes
Sales Director Melanie Wilkins
Head of Books Jennifer Goldstein
CEO and Founder Jelani Memory

DK
Delhi Technical Team Bimlesh Tiwary Pushpak Tyagi, Rakesh Kumar
Senior Production Editor Jennifer Murray
Senior Production Controller Louise Minihane
Senior Acquisitions Editor Katy Flint
Acquisitions Project Editor Sara Forster
Managing Art Editor Vicky Short
Managing Director, Licensing Mark Searle

First American edition, 2025
Published in the United States by DK Publishing, 1745 Broadway, 20th Floor,
New York, NY 10019

First published in Great Britain in 2025 by
Dorling Kindersley Limited, 20 Vauxhall Bridge Road, London SW1V 2SA
A Penguin Random House Company

The authorised representative in the EEA is
Dorling Kindersley Verlag GmbH. Arnulfstr. 124, 80636 Munich, Germany

A catalog record for this book is available from the Library of Congress.
A CIP catalogue record for this book is available from the British Library.
ISBN: 978-0-2417-4344-7

DK books are available at special discounts when purchased in bulk for sales
promotions, premiums, fund-raising, or education use. For details, contact:
DK Publishing Special Markets, 1745 Broadway, 20th Floor, New York, NY 10019
SpecialSales@dk.com

Printed and bound in China
www.dk.com
akidsco.com

For the children.

Intro
for grownups

We "grownups" do our best to teach kids as much as possible throughout their lives. For example, how to read, be nice to other people, and do the right thing. We hope to teach them even bigger things...like how to dream, how to show compassion, and how to admit when you're wrong. Ultimately, the most important thing we can teach them about is friendship.

So...what age is too young for kids to learn how to make friends, or what it takes to be a good friend? When is the "right" age for kids to learn about how to treat others? Who is supposed to help kids learn about friendship?

This is a book designed to get the conversation started. To help grownups and kids begin the discussion and hopefully continue to talk about friendship. Friendship is the most powerful thing in the world. Value it, nurture it, and let it enrich your heart and soul. Hope you enjoy the book!

Hey, there!

My name is Duncan.

And throughout my life, I've grown to believe 1 thing:

Friendship is the most important thing in the world!

Big claim, I know, but hear me out.

When I was younger, both of my parents struggled with drinking too much alcohol.

This meant they weren't always there for me or able to **take care of me**.

I often felt scared and alone.

But guess what?

Friendship **changed all of that** for me.

I used to play just about every sport:

baseball,
football,
basketball,
rugby,
golf.

It didn't matter what the sport was,
as long as it was with other people.

Sports weren't just
about playing fun games.

They were for spending time with
friends and **making new ones**.

We'd play all day, share stories, stand up for each other, and hang out until we had to go home.

Honestly, **friendship saved my life.**

But why is friendship **so important**?

Simple...

Humans are meant to connect.

It's in our **nature**.

nt for

ion.

Have you ever felt that warmth, that happiness, just being with someone?

That's friendship working its **magic**.

Friendship

is the bond that ties us together,
makes us laugh, and helps us
when times get tough.

We are most happy and most ourselves when we have others **we call friends**.

I'm proud to say that over my lifetime, I've made **a lot of friends**.

They have made my life wonderful, beautiful, and amazing!

But you might be wondering...

How do friendsh work?

Well, I've come up with
an equation for friendship.

es
ip

Want to hear it?!

Time +
Closene
x Authe
= Fr

ss
nticity
iendship.
That's it.
That's what makes a friendship.

First:

To be friends, you have
to spend **time** together.

This can mean watching movies, playing a game, talking on the phone—whatever you enjoy doing together.

Second:

To be friends, you have to add some **connection**.

This means just being around each other, sharing the same space in person or virtually.

Third:

To be friends, you have
to have **authenticity**.

This means the effects of the time and connection spent are multiplied the more you're just being yourself.

And guess what?

Friendship can happen with anyone!

Think about it.

Friends can be:

kids that live next door.

family members or siblings.

teachers, coaches,
or grownups in your life.

classmates, teammates,
and bandmates.

I bet you already have some
friends—can you name a
few of them right now?

The more time, space, and self you share with your friends, the deeper the friendship gets.

Friendships are like trees; they may start small, but with time and care, they grow tall and strong.

And here's the best part...

friend is powe

Friendship has the **power** to:

help you understand yourself better.

feel at peace, even in chaos.

build your self-confidence.

let you feel OK when you're down.

teach you about the world.

forgive, even when you mess up.

grow your courage.

create more resilience.

push you to be the best
version of yourself.

And friendship is sooooo much fun!

Powerful, isn't it?

But I want you to know that friendship is both a **choice** and a **commitment**.

It's about 2 people deciding to **be there for each other**.

Trusting, sharing, and understanding.

Not everyone will be your friend, and it's **OK** to choose not to be friends with someone.

It's always your choice.

And you'll know you have a true friend when they are there for you, **NO MATTER WHAT!**

So, how do you make new friends and grow deeper connections with the friends you already have?

Remember the 3 B's!

Be with them.

Quality time matters.

Be yourself.

Show your true colors, always.

Be together.

Cherish every moment.

And, it's **OK to have differences**. In fact, differences often make friendships better.

They can bring new
perspectives, stories, and joys.

So, as you journey through life, here's a few things to take to heart...

Friendship is the most powerful thing in the world.

Value it, nurture it, and let it enrich your heart and soul.

Here's to friendship, life's greatest gift!

Outro
for grownups

You've made it to the end of the book... congratulations! Now, what's next? The answer...more discussion, more ideas, and more friends! Kids may have a lot of questions like, "What makes a good friend?" or, "How can I be a good friend?" Make the most of their curiosity!

Talk about your own personal experience with friendship. Talk about friendship as both a choice and a commitment. Kids are ready, if only the grownups in their lives are willing to start the conversation. Here's to friendship, life's greatest gift!

About The Author

Duncan Campbell's (he/him) passion for helping society's most vulnerable children grew from his own experience as a youth living in inner city Portland. That eventually led him to found 3 children's organizations: The Children's Course, Children's Institute, and the nationally recognized organization, Friends of the Children.

Friends of the Children hires full-time, paid professional mentors called Friends who walk alongside each child for 12 or more years, from kindergarten through high school graduation, no matter what. Friends of the Children started with 16 children in 1993 and is now serving thousands of youth and families in 36 locations across the country.

**This book was created in partnership
with Friends of the Children.**

📷 @friendsnational, @friendspdx

f @friendsofthechildrennational, @friendspdx

🌐 friendsofthechildren.org, friendspdx.org

Made to empower.

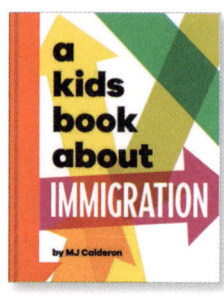

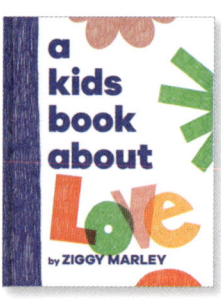

Discover more at akidsco.com